D0835974

500 315 760 82

✣ **Our** ✣
# Kings and Queens

# HENRY VIII

## Gill Munton

Based on an original text by
Katrina Siliprandi

**WAYLAND**

# Our Kings and Queens

## Titles in the series

## HENRY VIII
## VICTORIA

**Editor:** Jason Hook
**Original design:** Jean Wheeler
**Cover design:** Tessa Barwick
**Differentiated design:** Raynor Design
**Text consultant:** Norah Granger, University of Brighton

Based on an original text *Kings and Queens – Henry VIII*
by Katrina Siliprandi, published in 1995 by Wayland Publishers Limited

First published in 1998 by Wayland Publishers Limited, 61 Western Road, Hove, East Sussex BN3 1JD
© Copyright 1998 Wayland Publishers Limited
Find Wayland on the Internet at http://www.wayland.co.uk

**British Library Cataloguing in Publication Data**
Munton, Gill
Henry VIII. - (Our kings and queens)
1. Henry, VIII, King of England - Juvenile literature
2. Great Britain - Kings and rulers - Biography - Juvenile literature
3. Great Britain - History - Henry VIII, 1509-1547 - Juvenile literature
I. Title
942'.052'092
ISBN 0 7502 2280 8

Typeset in England by Raynor Design
Printed and bound by G. Canale & C.S.p.A, Turin, Italy
Cover picture: Henry VIII dressed to show his wealth and power.

## All Wayland books encourage children to read and help them improve their literacy.

- ✓ The contents page, page numbers, headings and index help locate specific pieces of information.
- ✓ The glossary reinforces alphabetic knowledge and extends vocabulary.
- ✓ The further information section suggests other books dealing with the same subject.
- ✓ Find out more about how this book is specifically relevant to the National Literacy Strategy on page 30.

# Contents

# Henry's Early Years

King Henry VIII had a strong navy. One of his warships was called the *Mary Rose*.

In 1545, Henry sent the *Mary Rose* into battle against French ships. Just after the ship had left Portsmouth, it began to fill up with water. The *Mary Rose* sank, and the crew of 500 men were drowned.

▼ This is a picture of the *Mary Rose*.

▲ Henry when he was a young boy.

◄ Henry when he was about thirty-six.

When he watched the sinking of the *Mary Rose*, Henry VIII had been king of England for thirty-six years.

## Henry's family

Henry was born on 28 June 1491. His father was King Henry VII, and his mother was Elizabeth of York. He had an elder brother called Arthur, and two sisters called Margaret and Mary. The four children grew up in palaces near London.

## Important Dates

**1491**
Henry was born.

**1509**
Henry became the king.

▲ This tapestry shows Arthur and Catherine of Aragon getting engaged.

## Arthur dies

Henry's elder brother, Arthur, married Catherine of Aragon when he was only fifteen. Catherine was the daughter of the king and queen of Spain. But Arthur died five months after the wedding.

After Arthur's death, Henry became Prince of Wales. He spent most of his time hunting, hawking and jousting. Henry also liked wrestling and archery.

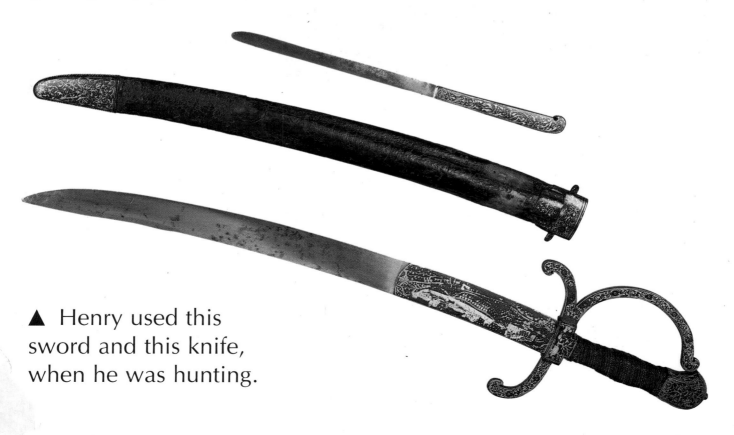

▲ Henry used this sword and this knife, when he was hunting.

◄ Henry wearing beautiful robes and expensive jewels.

Henry was tall with broad shoulders. He had a handsome face and long, red hair. He wore beautiful clothes to show people how rich and powerful he was.

Henry did very well at school. He learned to speak and write in four languages.

▶ A painting of Catherine of Aragon. She was the first wife of Henry VIII.

## Catherine of Aragon

Henry married Catherine of Aragon, the widow of Arthur, his brother. Catherine was a beautiful woman, with grey eyes and long, golden-brown hair. Henry and Catherine rode in a procession through London. Crowds of people cheered.

## Henry becomes king

Henry's father, Henry VII, died in 1509. Henry became king. He was seventeen. After Henry was crowned, there was a feast and a jousting tournament.

The new king had some of his father's ministers arrested. Two of them had made the people pay high taxes. Henry had them executed. This made him popular with the English people.

▲ Henry being crowned king at Westminster Abbey in London.

◄ Henry (far left) wearing a padded jacket. This made him look big and powerful.

# How Henry Ruled

The new king was very rich. He spent a lot of money on feasts, and he loved gambling with dice and cards.

Henry enjoyed hunting stags and boars. He also liked the sport of jousting.

Henry took part in his first jousting competition wearing a disguise. He did very well, and the crowd celebrated when they found out who he was.

▲ Henry returning from a jousting competition.

Henry liked writing music. He played the recorder and the virginals (an instrument like a small piano). Henry also liked to sing and dance. He had many musicians at his court.

Henry was sometimes too busy to think about being king. He did not like writing letters, or even reading them. His ministers had to do most of the work.

▲ Henry probably wrote this piece of music.

## Important Dates

**1513**
Henry fought wars with France and Scotland.

**1515**
Thomas Wolsey became Lord Chancellor.

**1520**
Henry went to France to meet King Francis I.

▲ This is Henry's writing desk.

► Henry had many servants to serve him his meals.

## Henry goes to war

Henry ruled England, Wales, part of Ireland and part of France. He wanted to rule the whole of France, so he got ready for war.

Henry spent a lot of money on his army and navy. Many warships were built during his reign. They included the *Great Harry*, which was the biggest ship in the world.

◄ Soldiers practising for war at a tournament.

Henry led an army to France in 1513. Three weeks later, he sent an army to Scotland. James IV of Scotland was killed in the fighting. But Henry never managed to defeat France or Scotland.

◀ Henry with his ministers in 1515.

▼ Henry's army attacking a town in France.

▲ Thomas Wolsey
wearing the robes
of a cardinal.

## Thomas Wolsey

Henry had many ministers to help him
run the country. The most important
minister was Thomas Wolsey. In 1515,
Henry made Wolsey his Lord Chancellor.

Although he was only the son of a
butcher, Wolsey became very rich and
powerful. He built a huge palace for
himself at Hampton Court. It had 1,000
rooms and 500 servants.

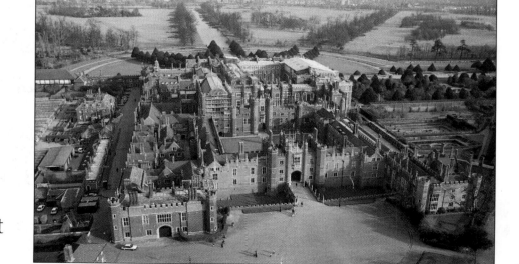

▶ You can still visit
Hampton Court.

▲ Henry VIII meeting Francis I, the king of France.

In 1515, Francis I became king of France. Henry thought of Francis as his rival, and tried to keep up with everything he did. He even grew a beard when he found out that Francis had one. In 1520, the two kings and their followers met in France.

▲ Francis I liked fine clothes as much as Henry.

# Henry and the Church

Most English people belonged to the Catholic Church. The head of this Church was the Pope.

In 1520, a German called Martin Luther wrote a book complaining about the Catholic Church. Henry wrote a book defending the Church.

## Important Dates

**1521**
Henry's book was published.

**1529**
Henry sacked Thomas Wolsey.

**1529**
Thomas More became Lord Chancellor.

**1533**
Henry secretly married Anne Boleyn.

**1536**
Anne Boleyn was executed. Henry married Jane Seymour.

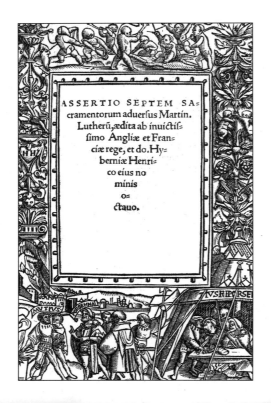

◄ This is the first page of Henry's book.

# Anne Boleyn

Henry and Catherine of Aragon had only one child, called Mary. Catherine could not have any more children. But Henry wanted a son, who could become the next king. He wanted to marry a young woman called Anne Boleyn.

## Wolsey is arrested

Henry decided to divorce Catherine. He told Wolsey to arrange this with the Pope. But the Pope would not agree.

Henry was furious. He blamed Wolsey, and had him arrested. Henry made Thomas More his new Lord Chancellor.

▲ Henry met Anne Boleyn in 1523. He fell in love with her.

◄ Henry sent Wolsey to London for trial, but he died on the journey.

▶ This picture shows Henry with the Archbishop of Canterbury, Thomas Cranmer.

## Henry takes control

As the Pope would not allow Henry to divorce Catherine, Henry took control of the Church in England. Henry made Thomas Cranmer his new Archbishop of Canterbury. He knew that Cranmer would let him divorce Catherine.

Cranmer ended Henry's marriage to Catherine. Anne Boleyn was crowned queen. Henry had already married her in secret. In 1533, she gave birth to a daughter, Elizabeth.

Henry ordered all the priests in England to look at their prayer books. He told them to cross out any words about the Pope. Henry was now the head of the English Church.

▲ This is Anne Boleyn's bedhead. She took it with her when she travelled.

◄ Thomas Cranmer was made Archbishop of Canterbury in 1533.

## A new law

Henry made a new law. It said that all English people had to read out an oath. This oath said that Henry, not the Pope, was now head of the English Church.

▲ Some people were burned to death if they refused to read Henry's oath.

People who would not read out the oath were executed. One of these people was Thomas More. Even though he was Lord Chancellor, he refused to read the oath.

# Anne Boleyn is executed

Henry still did not have a son. This made him very angry.

Henry thought that Anne Boleyn had other lovers. He put her in prison in the Tower of London. In 1536, Anne was executed. Ten days later, Henry married Jane Seymour.

▲ This axe and this block were used to execute people.

◄ Jane Seymour was Henry's third wife.

# Closing the Monasteries

There were about 600 monasteries in England. The monks and nuns who lived in them owned a great deal of land. Henry wanted this land. He looked for an excuse to close the monasteries.

Henry made Thomas Cromwell his new Lord Chancellor. Cromwell sent out inspectors to close the monasteries.

▲ This cartoon shows a monk as a greedy wolf.

## Important Dates

**1535**
Henry began to close the monasteries.

People in the north of England turned against Henry and Cromwell. They were angry about the closing of the monasteries. Henry ordered their leaders to be executed.

Henry was now very fat, and he had painful legs. He spent most of his time planning a new palace in Surrey, which was called Nonsuch.

▲ A drawing of Thomas Cromwell.

◄ This is a picture of Nonsuch Palace. Henry owned more than sixty houses and palaces.

▲ Castle Acre Priory in Norfolk was destroyed by Henry's inspectors.

All the monasteries were shut by the end of 1540. Henry took over the land, the buildings and the treasures inside the monasteries. He sold most of these treasures, and used the money to pay for his wars.

## Henry has a son

In 1537, Jane Seymour gave birth to a baby boy. Henry had a son at last. The new baby was called Edward.

# Jane Seymour dies

Henry now had a son who could become king when he died. But having a baby was dangerous in Tudor times. Doctors did not know as much as they do now.

Jane Seymour became very ill after the baby was born. She died soon afterwards from blood poisoning.

▲ This is Henry's son, Edward.

▼ This painting shows Henry and Jane Seymour with Edward, and Henry's two daughters, Mary and Elizabeth.

# Henry's Last Years

▲ A painting of Anne of Cleves.
She was Henry's fourth wife.

Cromwell arranged for Henry to marry Anne of Cleves. She was the daughter of a duke in northern Europe. Cromwell thought the marriage would give England some important friends in Europe.

Cromwell told Henry that Anne of Cleves was beautiful. But when Henry met Anne, he thought she was ugly.

Henry married Anne of Cleves in 1540. He divorced her the same year. Soon after this, Cromwell was executed.

Henry's next wife was Katherine Howard, one of Anne's servants. But Henry found out that Katherine had other lovers. He had her beheaded.

Henry married once more. His sixth wife, Katherine Parr, lived with him and his three children until he died.

▲ This window shows Henry with the badges of his six wives.

◄ Katherine Parr.

KATHARINE PARRE

## Important Dates

**1540**
Henry married Anne of Cleves.

Henry married Katherine Howard.

**1543**
Henry married Katherine Parr.

**1547**
Henry VIII died.

## At war again

Henry was now very fat. He could hardly walk, and his servants had to carry him everywhere. England was at war with France and Scotland again. The French tried to invade England. This is when the *Mary Rose* sank.

England and France made peace in 1546. The wars had used up all Henry's money. He ordered people to use less gold and silver for making coins, so he could keep it for himself.

◄ This suit of armour was made for Henry in 1540. It shows how fat he was.

◄ Henry when he was fifty-three years old.

▼ The last page of Henry VIII's will.

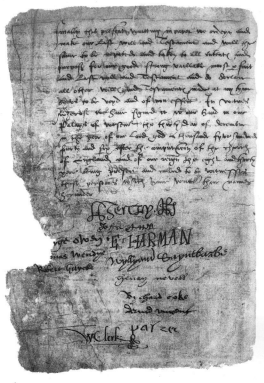

## Henry dies

Henry had been ill for a long time. He had painful legs and could not breathe easily. Henry was fifty-six years old when he died in 1547.

Henry's will made his young son Edward the next king of England.

# Glossary

**archery**  A sport using bows and arrows.

**bedhead**  The top of a bed.

**divorce**  The ending of a marriage by law.

**engaged**  Promised to be married.

**hawking**  A sport in which hawks are used to catch small animals or birds.

**jousting**  Fighting between two knights on horseback.

**Lord Chancellor**  The most important minister of a king or queen.

**minister**  An important member of a government.

**monasteries**  Places where monks or nuns live.

**oath**  A vow or promise.

**priory**  A type of monastery.

**tax**  Money which people have to pay to the government.

**tournament**  A fighting contest.

**widow**  A woman whose husband has died.

**will**  Instructions to be carried out after someone's death.

# Literacy Information

Children can use this book to improve their literacy skills in the following ways:

- ✓ They can identify the lists of dates in the panels, then locate the same information in the main text.
- ✓ They can use the headings to locate key pieces of information about the rule of Henry VIII.
- ✓ They can identify what they already know about Henry VIII, then verify and extend this knowledge using the book.
- ✓ Children can retell the strange facts about Henry's marriages in the form of a story.

# Books to Read

*Beware the King* by Stewart Ross (Evans, 1997)

*Great Lives – Henry VIII* by Dorothy Turner (Wayland, 1994)

*Tudor Monarchs* by Jessica Saraga (Batsford, 1992)

*Tudors* by Donna Bailey (Headway, 1993)

*What They Don't Tell You About Henry VIII* by Fred Finney (Hodder, 1995)

# Places to Visit

**Castle Acre Priory**, Castle Acre, King's Lynn, Norfolk
A monastery that was closed by Henry VIII.
**Hampton Court**, East Molesey, Surrey
The palace built by Cardinal Wolsey and taken over by Henry.
**The *Mary Rose***, HM Naval Base, Portsmouth
The remains of Henry's warship, named after his sister Mary.
**Tower of London**, London, EC3
This was used as a royal palace, then later as a prison.

**Picture acknowledgements**
The publishers would like to thank the following for permission to publish their pictures: The Bodleian Library 17 (bottom); The Bridgeman Art Library 5 (left, Fitzwilliam Museum, University of Cambridge), 8, 15 (bottom), 21 (bottom), 23 (top); The British Library 11 (top), 16; The College of Arms 10, 12 (bottom); E.T Archive 4 (Pepys Library, Magdalen College, Cambridge), 9 (bottom, by courtesy of Her Majesty the Queen), 12 (top, Trustees of the British Museum); Mary Evans 5 (right); Fotoatelier Gerhard Howald 22 (top); Fotomas Index 13 (bottom); Historic Royal Palaces (Crown Copyright) 21 (top), 27 (top); Jarrold Publishing 19 (top); Magdalen College, Oxford 6 (top); The Mansell Collection 13 (top), 15 (top), 18, 20, 22–3 (bottom), 29 (top); National Portrait Gallery *cover*, 7, 14 (top), 17 (top), 25 (top), 26, 27 (bottom); Norfolk Air Photographs Library (Derek A Edwards) 24; Public Record Office 29 (bottom); Royal Armouries 28; The Royal Collection © 1994 Her Majesty The Queen 6 (bottom), 25 (bottom); The President and Fellows of St. John's College, Oxford 26; Skyscan Balloon Photography 14 (bottom); Victoria and Albert Museum, courtesy of the Trustees of the V&A/P Barnard 11 (bottom); by courtesy of the Dean and Chapter of Westminster 9 (top).

# Index

Numbers in **bold** refer to pictures and captions.